Charles Seale-Hayne Library

University of Plymouth

(01752) 588 588

LibraryandITenquiries@plymouth.ac.uk

Cram101 Textbook Outlines to accompany:

Mathematics: A Human Endeavor

Jacobs, 3rd Edition

An Academic Internet Publishers (AIPI) publication (c) 2007.

You have a discounted membership at www.Cram101.com with this book.

Get all of the practice tests for the chapters of this textbook, and access in-depth reference material for writing essays and papers. Here is an example from a Cram101 Biology text:

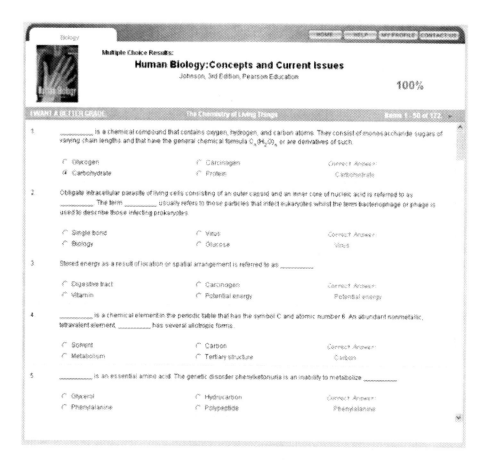

When you need problem solving help with math, stats, and other disciplines, www.Cram101.com will walk through the formulas and solutions step by step.

With Cram101.com online, you also have access to extensive reference material.

You will nail those essays and papers. Here is an example from a Cram101 Biology text:

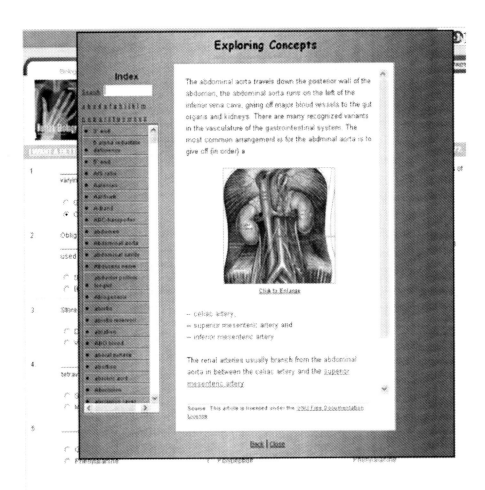

Visit **www.Cram101.com**, click Sign Up at the top of the screen, and enter DK73DW2046 in the promo code box on the registration screen. Access to www.Cram101.com is normally $9.95, but because you have purchased this book, your access fee is only $4.95. Sign up and stop highlighting textbooks forever.

Learning System

Cram101 Textbook Outlines is a learning system. The notes in this book are the highlights of your textbook, you will never have to highlight a book again.

How to use this book. Take this book to class, it is your notebook for the lecture. The notes and highlights on the left hand side of the pages follow the outline and order of the textbook. All you have to do is follow along while your intructor presents the lecture. Circle the items emphasized in class and add other important information on the right side. With Cram101 Textbook Outlines you'll spend less time writing and more time listening. Learning becomes more efficient.

Cram101.com Online

Increase your studying efficiency by using Cram101.com's practice tests and online reference material. It is the perfect complement to Cram101 Textbook Outlines. Use self-teaching matching tests or simulate in-class testing with comprehensive multiple choice tests, or simply use Cram's true and false tests for quick review. Cram101.com even allows you to enter your in-class notes for an integrated studying format combining the textbook notes with your class notes.

Visit **www.Cram101.com**, click Sign Up at the top of the screen, and enter **DK73DW2046** in the promo code box on the registration screen. Access to www.Cram101.com is normally $9.95, but because you have purchased this book, your access fee is only $4.95. Sign up and stop highlighting textbooks forever.

Mathematics: A Human Endeavor
Jacobs, 3rd

CONTENTS

Edward Kasner	Edward Kasner who studied under Cassius Jackson Keyser, was a prominent Jewish American mathematician who was appointed Tutor on Mathematics in the Columbia University Mathematics Department. Kasner was the first Jew appointed to a faculty position in the sciences at Columbia University.
Of the world	The population of the world is the total number of human beings alive on the planet Earth at a given time.
Diagram	A diagram is a simplified and structured visual representation of concepts, ideas, constructions, relations, statistical data, anatomy etc used in all aspects of human activities to visualize and clarify the topic.
Travel	Travel is the transport of people on a trip/journey or the process or time involved in a person or object moving from one location to another.
Square	In plane geometry, a square is a polygon with four equal sides, four right angles, and parallel opposite sides. In algebra, the square of a number is that number multiplied by itself.
Segment	In geometry, a line segment is a part of a line that is bounded by two end points, and contains every point on the line between its end points.
Units	The units of measurement are a globally standardized and modernized form of the metric system.
Center	In geometry, the center of an object is a point in some sense in the middle of the object.
Scale	In Euclidean geometry, a uniform scale is a linear transformation that enlargers or diminishes objects, and whose scale factor is the same in all directions. This is also called homothety.
Test	Acid test ratio measures the ability of a company to use its near cash or quick assets to immediately extinguish its current liabilities.
Truth	There are two main approaches to truth in mathematics. They are the model theory of truth and the proof theory of truth.
Reasoning	Deductive reasoning is the kind of reasoning in which the conclusion is necessitated by, or reached from, previously known facts (the premises).
Inductive	In mathematics, for a statement to be mathematically inductive, such a statement must be true of all natural numbers.
Inductive reasoning	Induction or inductive reasoning, sometimes called inductive logic, is the process of reasoning in which the premises of an argument are believed to support the conclusion but do not ensure it.
Data	Data is a synonym for information.
Measurement	Measurement is the estimation of a physical quantity such as distance, energy, temperature, or time.
Map	A map, is a symbolized depiction of space which highlights relations between components of that space. Most usually a map is a two-dimensional, geometrically accurate representation of a three-dimensional space.
Conclusion	In a mathematical proof or a syllogism, a conclusion is a statement that is the logical consequence of preceding statements.
Whole number	In mathematics, a whole number can mean either an element of the set {1, 2, 3, ...} (i.e the positive integers) or an element of the set {0, 1, 2, 3, ...} (i.e. the non-negative integers).
Pendulum	A pendulum is an object that is attached to a pivot point so that it can swing freely.
Galileo Galilei	Galileo Galilei was an Italian physicist, mathematician, astronomer, and philosopher who is closely associated with the scientific revolution.
Series	A series is the sum of the elements of a sequence.
Experiment	In the scientific method, an experiment (Latin: ex-+-periri, "of (or from) trying"), is a set of

actions and observations, performed in the context of solving a particular problem or question, in order to support or falsify a hypothesis or research concerning phenomena.

Volume
The volume of a solid object is the three-dimensional concept of how much space it occupies, often quantified numerically.

Planet
A planet, as defined by the International Astronomical Union , is a celestial body orbiting a star or stellar remnant that is massive enough to be rounded by its own gravity, not massive enough to cause thermonuclear fusion in its core, and has cleared its neighboring region of planetesimals.

Mean
The mean, the average in everyday English, which is also called the arithmetic mean (and is distinguished from the geometric mean or harmonic mean). The average is also called the sample mean. The expected value of a random variable, which is also called the population mean.

Asteroid
An Asteroid, also called a minor planet or planetoid, comes from a class of atsronomical objects.

Amount
amount is a kind of property which exists as magnitude or multitude. It is among the basic classes of things along with quality, substance, change, and relation.

Element
An element or member of a set is an object that when collected together make up the set.

Compound
Compound interest refers to the fact that whenever interest is calculated, it is based not only on the original principal, but also on any unpaid interest that has been added to the principal.

Elements
In mathematics, the elements , or members of a set or more generally a class are all those objects which when collected together make up the set or class.

Deductive reasoning
Deductive reasoning is the kind of reasoning in which the conclusion is necessitated by, or reached from, previously known facts (the premises).

Circle
In Euclidean geometry, a circle is the set of all points in a plane at a fixed distance, called the radius, from a given point, the center.

Line segment
A line segment is a part of a line that is bounded by two end points, and contains every point on the line between its end points.

Drawings
Drawings (i.e. Plans) are a set of two-dimensional diagrams or drawings used to describe a place or object, or to communicate building or fabrication instructions.

Rectangle
In geometry, a rectangle is defined as a quadrilateral where all four of its angles are right angles.

Proof
In mathematics, a proof is a demonstration that, assuming certain axioms, some statement is necessarily true.

Cube
A cube is a three-dimensional solid object bounded by six square faces, facets, or sides, with three meeting at each vertex.

Cubes
Cubes are of a number n in its third power-the result of multiplying it by itself three times.

Martin Gardner
Martin Gardner (b. October 21, 1914, Tulsa, Oklahoma) is a popular American mathematics and science writer specializing in recreational mathematics, but with interests encompassing magic (conjuring), pseudoscience, literature (especially Lewis Carroll), philosophy, and religion.

Statement
In common philosophical language, a proposition or statement, is the content of an assertion, that is, it is true-or-false and defined by the meaning of a particular piece of language.

Theorem
In mathematics, a theorem is a statement that can be proved on the basis of explicitly stated or previously agreed assumptions.

Logic
Mathematical logic really refers to two distinct areas of research: the first is the application of the techniques of formal logic to mathematics and mathematical reasoning, and the second, in the other direction, the application of mathematical techniques to the representation and analysis of formal logic.

Triangle	A triangle is one of the basic shapes of geometry: a polygon with three vertices and three sides which are straight line segments.
Pythagorean Theorem	Pythagorean Theorem is a relation in Euclidean geometry among the three sides of a right triangle.
Legs	In a right triangle, the legs of the triangle are the two sides that are perpendicular to each other, as opposed to the hypotenuse.
Hypotenuse	The hypotenuse of a right triangle is the triangle's longest side; the side opposite the right angle.
Right triangle	Right triangle has one 90° internal angle a right angle.
Shapes	Shapes are external two-dimensional outlines, with the appearance or configuration of some thing - in contrast to the matter or content or substance of which it is composed.
Translation	In Euclidean geometry, a translation is moving every point a constant distance in a specified direction.
Egyptian	The system of Egyptian numerals was a numeral system used in ancient Egypt. It was a decimal system, often rounded off to the higher power, written in hieroglyphs.
Degree	In mathematics, there are several meanings of degree depending on the subject.
Power	Power has many meanings, most of which simply .
Column	In mathematics, a matrix can be thought of as each row or column being a vector. Hence, a space formed by row vectors or column vectors are said to be a row space or a column space.
Numeral	A numeral is a symbol or group of symbols, or a word in a natural language that represents a number.
Proofs	Mathematical proofs are demonstrations that,assuming certain axioms, some statement is necessarily true.
Symbols	Symbols are objects, characters, or other concrete representations of ideas, concepts, or other abstractions.
Prime number	Prime number is a natural number that has exactly two distinct natural number divisors, which are 1 and the prime number itself.
Prime	In mathematics, a prime number (or a prime) is a natural number that has exactly two (distinct) natural number divisors, which are 1 and the prime number itself.
Sum	A sum is the result of the addition of a set of numbers. The numbers may be natural numbers, complex numbers, matrices, or still more complicated objects. An infinite sum is a subtle procedure known as a series.
Greatest common	In mathematics, the greatest common divisor of two non-zero integers, is the largest positive integer that divides both numbers without remainder.
Divisor	In mathematics, a divisor of an integer n, also called a factor of n, is an integer which evenly divides n without leaving a remainder.
Overhead	In business, overhead, overhead cost or overhead expense refers to an ongoing expense of operating a business.
Light	Light is electromagnetic radiation with a wavelength that is visible to the eye (visible light) or, in a technical or scientific context, electromagnetic radiation of any wavelength.
Donald Knuth	Donald Knuth is a renowned computer scientist and Professor Emeritus of the Art of Computer Programming at Stanford University.
Force	In physics, force is an influence that may cause an object to accelerate. It may be experienced as a

Go to **Cram101.com** for the Practice Tests for this Chapter.

Go to **Cram101.com** for the Practice Tests for this Chapter.
And, **NEVER** highlight a book again!

lift, a push, or a pull. The actual acceleration of the body is determined by the vector sum of all forces acting on it, known as net force or resultant force.

Turn   A turn is 360° or 2ð radians.

Go to **Cram101.com** for the Practice Tests for this Chapter.

Sequence	In mathematics, a sequence is an ordered list of objects. Like a set, it contains members, also called elements or terms, and the number of terms is called the length of the sequence. Unlike a set, order matters, and the exact same elements can appear multiple times at different positions in the sequence.
Counting	Counting is the mathematical action of repeatedly adding or subtracting one, usually to find out how many objects there are or to set aside a desired number of objects.
Arithmetic	Arithmetic or arithmetics is the oldest and most elementary branch of mathematics, used by almost everyone, for tasks ranging from simple daily counting to advanced science and business calculations.
Arithmetic sequence	Arithmetic sequence is a sequence of numbers such that the difference of any two successive members of the sequence is a constant.
Ellipsis	Ellipsis (plural ellipses; from Greek λλειψις 'omission face=symbol>¢) in linguistics refers to any omitted part of speech that is understood; i.e. the omission is intentional.
Expression	An expression is a combination of numbers, operators, grouping symbols and/or free variables and bound variables arranged in a meaningful way which can be evaluated..
Pyramid	An n-sided pyramid is a polyhedron formed by connecting an n-sided polygonal base and a point, called the apex, by n triangular faces. In other words, it is a conic solid with polygonal base.
Investment	Investment or investing is a term with several closely-related meanings in business management, finance and economics, related to saving or deferring consumption.
Geometric sequence	A geometric sequence is a sequence of numbers where each term after the first is found by multiplying the previous one by a fixed non-zero number called the common ratio.
Depression	A recession (i.e. depression) is traditionally defined in macroeconomics as a decline in a country's real Gross Domestic Product (GDP) for two or more successive quarters of a year (equivalently, two consecutive quarters of negative real economic growth).
Greater than	In mathematics, an inequality is a statement about the relative size or order of two objects. For example 14 > 10, or 14 is greater than 10.
Rate	A rate is a special kind of ratio, indicating a relationship between two measurements with different units, such as miles to gallons or cents to pounds.
Ratio	A ratio is a quantity that denotes the proportional amount or magnitude of one quantity relative to another.
Square	In plane geometry, a square is a polygon with four equal sides, four right angles, and parallel opposite sides. In algebra, the square of a number is that number multiplied by itself.
Sum	A sum is the result of the addition of a set of numbers. The numbers may be natural numbers, complex numbers, matrices, or still more complicated objects. An infinite sum is a subtle procedure known as a series.
Numeral	A numeral is a symbol or group of symbols, or a word in a natural language that represents a number.
Units	The units of measurement are a globally standardized and modernized form of the metric system.
Code	In mathematical logic, a Gödel numbering (or Gödel code) is a function that assigns to each

Go to **Cram101.com** for the Practice Tests for this Chapter.

Go to **Cram101.com** for the Practice Tests for this Chapter.
And, **NEVER** highlight a book again!

	symbol and well-formed formula of some formal language a unique natural number called its Gödel number.
Leibniz	Leibniz was a German mathematician and philosopher. He invented calculus independently of Newton, and his notation is the one in general use since.
Solid	In mathematics, solid geometry was the traditional name for the geometry of three-dimensional Euclidean space — for practical purposes the kind of space we live in.
Babylonian	A Babylonian was a citizen of Babylonia, named for its capital city, Babylon, which was an ancient state in the south part of Mesopotamia (in modern Iraq), combining the territories of Sumer and Akkad.
Square numbers	In mathematics, square numbers, sometimes called perfect squares, are integers that can be written as the square of some other integer; in other words, it is the product of some integer with itself.
Array	In computer science an array is a data structure that consists of a group of elements having a single name that are accessed by indexing. In most programming languages each element has the same data type and the array occupies a continuous area of storage.
Square root	In mathematics, a square root of a number x is a number r such that $r^2 = x$, or in words, a number r whose square (the result of multiplying the number by itself) is x.
Symbols	Symbols are objects, characters, or other concrete representations of ideas, concepts, or other abstractions.
Root	In mathematics, a root of a complex-valued function f is a member x of the domain of f such that f(x) vanishes at x, that is, $x : f(x) = 0$.
Consecutive	Consecutive means in succession or back-to-back
Acceleration	Acceleration is defined as the rate of change or derivative with respect to time of velocity.
Meter	The metre (or meter, see spelling differences) is a measure of length. It is the basic unit of length in the metric system and in the International System of Units (SI), used around the world for general and scientific purposes.
Linear	The word linear comes from the Latin word linearis, which means created by lines.
Perimeter	Perimeter is the distance around a given two-dimensional object. As a general rule, the perimeter of a polygon can always be calculated by adding all the length of the sides together. So, the formula for triangles is P = a + b + c, where a, b and c stand for each side of it. For quadrilaterals the equation is P = a + b + c + d. For equilateral polygons, P = na, where n is the number of sides and a is the side length.
Element	An element or member of a set is an object that when collected together make up the set.
Elements	In mathematics, the elements , or members of a set or more generally a class are all those objects which when collected together make up the set or class.
Subgroup	In group theory, given a group G under a binary operation *, we say that some subset H of G is a subgroup of G if H also forms a group under the operation *.
Cube	A cube is a three-dimensional solid object bounded by six square faces, facets, or sides, with three meeting at each vertex.
Cubes	Cubes are of a number n in its third power-the result of multiplying it by itself three times.
Volume	The volume of a solid object is the three-dimensional concept of how much space it occupies, often quantified numerically.

Power	Power has many meanings, most of which simply .
Cubic units	Cubic units are cubes in which all sides are of the same length and all face perpendicular to each other including an atom at each corner of the unigt cell.
Column	In mathematics, a matrix can be thought of as each row or column being a vector. Hence, a space formed by row vectors or column vectors are said to be a row space or a column space.
Diameter	In geometry, a diameter (Greek words diairo = divide and metro = measure) of a circle is any straight line segment that passes through the centre and whose endpoints are on the circular boundary, or, in more modern usage, the length of such a line segment. When using the word in the more modern sense, one speaks of the diameter rather than a diameter, because all diameters of a circle have the same length. This length is twice the radius. The diameter of a circle is also the longest chord that the circle has.
Amount	amount is a kind of property which exists as magnitude or multitude. It is among the basic classes of things along with quality, substance, change, and relation.
Exponentiating	Exponentiating is a mathematical operation, written a^n, involving two numbers, the base a and the exponent n.
Exponentiation	Exponentiation is a mathematical operation, written a^n, involving two numbers, the base a and the exponent n.
Construction	Compass and straightedge or ruler-and-compass construction is the construction of lengths or angles using only an idealized ruler and compass.
Fibonacci	Leonardo of Pisa (1170s or 1180s – 1250), also known as Leonardo Pisano, Leonardo Bonacci, Leonardo Fibonacci, or, most commonly, simply Fibonacci, was an Italian mathematician, considered by some "the most talented mathematician of the Middle Ages."
Algebra	Algebra is a branch of mathematics concerning the study of structure, relation and quantity.
Pairs	In mathematics, the conjugate pairs or adjoint matrix of an m-by-n matrix A with complex entries is the n-by-m matrix A* obtained from A by taking the transpose and then taking the complex conjugate of each entry.
Data	Data is a synonym for information.
Roman	Roman numerals are a numeral system originating in ancient Rome, adapted from Etruscan numerals.
Scale	In Euclidean geometry, a uniform scale is a linear transformation that enlargers or diminishes objects, and whose scale factor is the same in all directions. This is also called homothethy.
Cone	A cone is a three-dimensional geometric shape formed by straight lines through a fixed point (vertex) to the points of a fixed curve (directrix)
Divisor	In mathematics, a divisor of an integer n, also called a factor of n, is an integer which evenly divides n without leaving a remainder.
Reasoning	Deductive reasoning is the kind of reasoning in which the conclusion is necessitated by, or reached from, previously known facts (the premises).
Measure	A measure is a function that assigns a number to subsets of a given set.
Ruler	A ruler is an instrument used in geometry technical drawing and engineering/building to measure distances and/or to rule straight lines.
Rhind papyrus	The Rhind Papyrus , is named after Alexander Henry Rhind, a Scottish antiquarian, who purchased the papyrus in 1858 in Luxor, Egypt; it was apparently found during illegal

Go to **Cram101.com** for the Practice Tests for this Chapter.

excavations in or near the Ramesseum.

Spectrum	A spectrum is a condition or value that is not limited to a specific set of values but can vary infinitely within a continuum.
Mean	The mean, the average in everyday English, which is also called the arithmetic mean (and is distinguished from the geometric mean or harmonic mean). The average is also called the sample mean. The expected value of a random variable, which is also called the population mean.
Bar	The bar (symbol bar) and the millibar (symbol mbar, also mb) are units of pressure.
Factorial	Factorial of a non-negative integer n is the product of all positive integers less than or equal to n.
Gallon	U.S. liquid gallon is legally defined as 231 cubic inches, and is equal to 3.785411784 litres or abotu 0.13368 cubic feet. This is the most common definition of a gallon. The U.S. fluid ounce is defined as 1/128 of a U.S. gallon.
Space	Space is a set, with some particular properties and usually some additional structure, such as the operations of addition or multiplication, for instance.
Turn	A turn is 360° or 2ð radians.
Slide	The slide rule, also known as a slipstick, is a mechanical analog computer, consisting of at least two finely divided scales , most often a fixed outer pair and a movable inner one, with a sliding window called the cursor.
Mile	A mile is a unit of length, usually used to measure distance, in a number of different systems, including Imperial units, United States customary units and Norwegian/Swedish mil. Its size can vary from system to system, but in each is between 1 and 10 kilometers. In contemporary English contexts mile refers to either:
Palindrome	A palindrome is a word, phrase, number or other sequences of units that has the property of reading the same in either direction .
Theorem	In mathematics, a theorem is a statement that can be proved on the basis of explicitly stated or previously agreed assumptions.
Proof	In mathematics, a proof is a demonstration that, assuming certain axioms, some statement is necessarily true.
Proofs	Mathematical proofs are demonstrations that,assuming certain axioms, some statement is necessarily true.
Travel	Travel is the transport of people on a trip/journey or the process or time involved in a person or object moving from one location to another.
Johannes Kepler	Johannes Kepler was a German Lutheran mathematician, astronomer and astrologer, and a key figure in the 17th century astronomical revolution.
Period	In business, particularly accounting, a period is the time intervals that the accounts, statement, payments, or other calculations cover.
Planet	A planet, as defined by the International Astronomical Union , is a celestial body orbiting a star or stellar remnant that is massive enough to be rounded by its own gravity, not massive enough to cause thermonuclear fusion in its core, and has cleared its neighboring region of planetesimals.
Calculation	A calculation is a deliberate process for transforming one or more inputs into one or more results.

Go to **Cram101.com** for the Practice Tests for this Chapter.

Graphs	Graphs are the basic objects of study in graph theory. Informally speaking, a graph is a set of objects called points, nodes, or vertices connected by links called lines or edges.
Function	The mathematical concept of a function expresses the intuitive idea of deterministic dependence between two quantities, one of which is viewed as primary and the other as secondary. A function then is a way to associate a unique output for each input of a specified type, for example, a real number or an element of a given set.
Rate	A rate is a special kind of ratio, indicating a relationship between two measurements with different units, such as miles to gallons or cents to pounds.
Temperature	Temperature is a physical property of a system that underlies the common notions of hot and cold; something that is hotter has the greater temperature.
Variable	A variable is a symbolic representation denoting a quantity or expression. It often represents an "unknown" quantity that has the potential to change.
Fahrenheit	Fahrenheit is a temperature scale named after the German physicist Daniel Gabriel Fahrenheit , who proposed it in 1724.
Degree	In mathematics, there are several meanings of degree depending on the subject.
Sequence	In mathematics, a sequence is an ordered list of objects. Like a set, it contains members, also called elements or terms, and the number of terms is called the length of the sequence. Unlike a set, order matters, and the exact same elements can appear multiple times at different positions in the sequence.
Geometric sequence	A geometric sequence is a sequence of numbers where each term after the first is found by multiplying the previous one by a fixed non-zero number called the common ratio.
Cylinder	In mathematics, a cylinder is a quadric surface, with the following equation in Cartesian coordinates: $(x/_a)^2 + (y/_b)^2 = 1$.
Mile	A mile is a unit of length, usually used to measure distance, in a number of different systems, including Imperial units, United States customary units and Norwegian/Swedish mil. Its size can vary from system to system, but in each is between 1 and 10 kilometers. In contemporary English contexts mile refers to either:
Gallon	U.S. liquid gallon is legally defined as 231 cubic inches, and is equal to 3.785411784 litres or abotu 0.13368 cubic feet. This is the most common definition of a gallon. The U.S. fluid ounce is defined as 1/128 of a U.S. gallon.
Algebra	Algebra is a branch of mathematics concerning the study of structure, relation and quantity.
Descartes	Descartes was a highly influential French philosopher, mathematician, scientist, and writer. Dubbed the "Founder of Modern Philosophy", and the "Father of Modern Mathematics". His theories provided the basis for the calculus of Newton and Leibniz, by applying infinitesimal calculus to the tangent line problem, thus permitting the evolution of that branch of modern mathematics
Probability	Probability is the chance that something is likely to happen or be the case.
Pascal	Blaise Pascal was a French mathematician, physicist, and religious philosopher.
Galileo Galilei	Galileo Galilei was an Italian physicist, mathematician, astronomer, and philosopher who is closely associated with the scientific revolution.
Universal	Universal algebra (sometimes called General algebra) is the field of mathematics that studies the ideas common to all algebraic structures.
Reasoning	Deductive reasoning is the kind of reasoning in which the conclusion is necessitated by, or reached from, previously known facts (the premises).

Go to **Cram101.com** for the Practice Tests for this Chapter.

Truth	There are two main approaches to truth in mathematics. They are the model theory of truth and the proof theory of truth.
Coordinate	A coordinate is a set of numbers that designate location in a given reference system, such as x,y in a planar coordinate system or an x,y,z in a three-dimensional coordinate system.
Analytic geometry	Analytic geometry is the study of geometry using the principles of algebra. Analytic geometry can be explained more simply: it is concerned with defining geometrical shapes in a numerical way and extracting numerical information from that representation.
Perpendicular	In geometry, two lines or planes if one falls on the other in such a way as to create congruent adjacent angles. The term may be used as a noun or adjective. Thus, referring to Figure 1, the line AB is the perpendicular to CD through the point B.
Plane	In mathematics, a plane is a two-dimensional manifold or surface that is perfectly flat.
Origin	In mathematics, the origin of a coordinate system is the point where the axes of the system intersect.
Axes	An axes is when two lines intersect somewhere on a plane creating a right angle at intersection
Interval	In elementary algebra, an interval is a set that contains every real number between two indicated numbers and may contain the two numbers themselves.
Negative number	A negative number is a number that is less than zero.
Hyperbola	In mathematics, a hyperbola is a type of conic section defined as the intersection between a right circular conical surface and a plane which cuts through both halves of the cone.
Parabola	In mathematics, the parabola is a conic section generated by the intersection of a right circular conical surface and a plane parallel to a generating straight line of that surface. It can also be defined as locus of points in a plane which are equidistant from a given point.
Axis	An axis is a straight line around which a geometric figure can be rotated.
Average	In mathematics, an average, mean, or central tendency of a data set refers to a measure of the "middle" or "expected" value of the data set.
Measure	A measure is a function that assigns a number to subsets of a given set.
Amount	amount is a kind of property which exists as magnitude or multitude. It is among the basic classes of things along with quality, substance, change, and relation.
Units	The units of measurement are a globally standardized and modernized form of the metric system.
Travel	Travel is the transport of people on a trip/journey or the process or time involved in a person or object moving from one location to another.
Miles per hour	Miles per hour is a unit of speed, expressing the number of international miles covered per hour.
Celsius	Celsius is, or relates to, the Celsius temperature scale .
Metric	In mathematics a metric is a function which defines a distance between elements of a set.
Metric system	The metric system is a decimalized system of measurement based on the metre and the gram.
Curve	In mathematics, the concept of a curve tries to capture the intuitive idea of a geometrical one-dimensional and continuous object. A simple example is the circle.
Scale	In Euclidean geometry, a uniform scale is a linear transformation that enlargers or

Go to **Cram101.com** for the Practice Tests for this Chapter.

diminishes objects, and whose scale factor is the same in all directions. This is also called homothethy.

Product	In mathematics, a product is the result of multiplying, or an expression that identifies factors to be multiplied.
Square	In plane geometry, a square is a polygon with four equal sides, four right angles, and parallel opposite sides. In algebra, the square of a number is that number multiplied by itself.
Diameter	In geometry, a diameter (Greek words diairo = divide and metro = measure) of a circle is any straight line segment that passes through the centre and whose endpoints are on the circular boundary, or, in more modern usage, the length of such a line segment. When using the word in the more modern sense, one speaks of the diameter rather than a diameter, because all diameters of a circle have the same length. This length is twice the radius. The diameter of a circle is also the longest chord that the circle has.
Minutes	Minutes are a measure of time.
Cube	A cube is a three-dimensional solid object bounded by six square faces, facets, or sides, with three meeting at each vertex.
Sound wave	Sound is a disturbance of mechanical energy that propagates through matter as a wave or sound wave.
Frequency	In statistics the frequency of an event i is the number n_i of times the event occurred in the experiment or the study. These frequencies are often graphically represented in histograms.
Meter	The metre (or meter, see spelling differences) is a measure of length. It is the basic unit of length in the metric system and in the International System of Units (SI), used around the world for general and scientific purposes.
Volume	The volume of a solid object is the three-dimensional concept of how much space it occupies, often quantified numerically.
Extrapolation	In mathematics, extrapolation is the process of constructing new data points outside a discrete set of known data points. It is similar to the process of interpolation, which constructs new points between known points, but its results are often less meaningful, and are subject to greater uncertainty.
Interpolation	Interpolation is a method of constructing new data points from a discrete set of known data points.
Prediction	A prediction is a statement or claimt that a particular event will occur in the future in more certain terms than a forecast.
Curves	In mathematics, curves are the intuitive idea of a geometrical one-dimensional and continuous object.
Direct	In mathematics and logic, a direct proof is a way of showing the truth or falsehood of a given statement by a straightforward combination of established facts, usually existing lemmas and theorems, without making any further assumptions.
Wholesale	According to the United Nations Statistics Division, Wholesale is the resale sale without transformation of new and used goods to retailers, to industrial, commercial, institutional or professional users, or to other wholesalers, or involves acting as an agent or broker in buying merchandise for, or selling merchandise, to such persons or companies.
Returns	Returns, in economics and political economy, are the distributions or payments awarded to the various suppliers of the factors of production.

Go to **Cram101.com** for the Practice Tests for this Chapter.

Conjecture	In mathematics, a conjecture is a mathematical statement which appears likely to be true, but has not been formally proven to be true under the rules of mathematical logic.
Investment	Investment or investing is a term with several closely-related meanings in business management, finance and economics, related to saving or deferring consumption.
Kilogram	The kilogram or kilogramme is the SI base unit of mass. It is defined as being equal to the mass of the international prototype of the kilogram.
Graph of a function	In mathematics, the graph of a function f is the collection of all ordered pairs . In particular, graph means the graphical representation of this collection, in the form of a curve or surface, together with axes, etc. Graphing on a Cartesian plane is sometimes referred to as curve sketching.
Buoyancy	In physics, buoyancy is the upward force on an object produced by the surrounding fluid in which it is fully or partially immersed, due to the pressure difference of the fluid between the top and bottom of the object.
Knot	A knot is a method for fastening or securing linear material such as rope by tying or interweaving. It may consist of a length of one or more segments of rope, string, webbing, twine, strap or even chain interwoven so as to create in the line the ability to bind to itself or to some other object - the "load". Knots have been the subject of interest both for their ancient origins, common use, and the mathematical implications of knot theory.
Equator	The equator is an imaginary line on the Earth's surface equidistant from the North Pole and South Pole.
Center	In geometry, the center of an object is a point in some sense in the middle of the object.
Radius	In classical geometry, a radius of a circle or sphere is any line segment from its center to its boundary. By extension, the radius of a circle or sphere is the length of any such segment. The radius is half the diameter. In science and engineering the term radius of curvature is commonly used as a synonym for radius.
Legs	In a right triangle, the legs of the triangle are the two sides that are perpendicular to each other, as opposed to the hypotenuse.
Circle	In Euclidean geometry, a circle is the set of all points in a plane at a fixed distance, called the radius, from a given point, the center.
Shapes	Shapes are external two-dimensional outlines, with the appearance or configuration of some thing - in contrast to the matter or content or substance of which it is composed.
Series	A series is the sum of the elements of a sequence.
Horizontal	In astronomy, geography, geometry and related sciences and contexts, a plane is said to be horizontal at a given point if it is locally perpendicular to the gradient of the gravity field, i.e., with the direction of the gravitational force at that point.
Light	Light is electromagnetic radiation with a wavelength that is visible to the eye (visible light) or, in a technical or scientific context, electromagnetic radiation of any wavelength.
Ratio	A ratio is a quantity that denotes the proportional amount or magnitude of one quantity relative to another.
Population	In sociology and biology a population is the collection of people or organisms of a particular species living in a given geographic area or space, usually measured by a census.
Space	Space is a set, with some particular properties and usually some additional structure, such as the operations of addition or multiplication, for instance.
Universe	The Universe is defined as the summation of all particles and energy that exist and the space-

Go to **Cram101.com** for the Practice Tests for this Chapter.

25

time which all events occur.

Go to **Cram101.com** for the Practice Tests for this Chapter.

Exponentiating	Exponentiating is a mathematical operation, written a^n, involving two numbers, the base a and the exponent n.
Exponentiation	Exponentiation is a mathematical operation, written a^n, involving two numbers, the base a and the exponent n.
Power	Power has many meanings, most of which simply .
Exponential	In mathematics, exponential growth occurs when the growth rate of a function is always proportional to the function's current size.
Star	In star algebra, a *-ring is an associative ring with an antilinear, antiautomorphism * : A ¨ A which is an involution.
Universe	The Universe is defined as the summation of all particles and energy that exist and the space-time which all events occur.
Multiplication	In mathematics, multiplication is an elementary arithmetic operation. When one of the numbers is a whole number, multiplication is the repeated sum of the other number.
Arithmetic	Arithmetic or arithmetics is the oldest and most elementary branch of mathematics, used by almost everyone, for tasks ranging from simple daily counting to advanced science and business calculations.
Edward Kasner	Edward Kasner who studied under Cassius Jackson Keyser, was a prominent Jewish American mathematician who was appointed Tutor on Mathematics in the Columbia University Mathematics Department. Kasner was the first Jew appointed to a faculty position in the sciences at Columbia University.
Googol	A googol is the large number 10100, that is, the digit 1 followed by one hundred zeros.
Archimedes	Archimedes of Syracuse was an ancient Greek mathematician, physicist and engineer. In addition to making important discoveries in the field of mathematics and geometry, he is credited with producing machines that were well ahead of their time.
Mean	The mean, the average in everyday English, which is also called the arithmetic mean (and is distinguished from the geometric mean or harmonic mean). The average is also called the sample mean. The expected value of a random variable, which is also called the population mean.
Notation	Mathematical notation is used to represent ideas.
Mass	Mass is the property of a physical object that quantifies the amount of matter and energy it is equivalent to.
Scientific notation	Scientific notation is a notation for writing numbers that is often used by scientists and mathematicians to make it easier to write large and small numbers.
Galileo Galilei	Galileo Galilei was an Italian physicist, mathematician, astronomer, and philosopher who is closely associated with the scientific revolution.
Center	In geometry, the center of an object is a point in some sense in the middle of the object.
Kilometer	A kilometer is a unit of length in the metric system, equal to one thousand metres, the current SI base unit of length
Coefficient	In mathematics, a coefficient is a constant multiplicative factor of a certain object. The object can be such things as a variable, a vector, a function, etc. For example, the coefficient of $9x^2$ is 9.
Decimal point	The decimal separator is a symbol used to mark the boundary between the integral and the fractional parts of a decimal numeral. Terms implying the symbol used are decimal point and

Go to **Cram101.com** for the Practice Tests for this Chapter.

decimal comma.

Kilogram	The kilogram or kilogramme is the SI base unit of mass. It is defined as being equal to the mass of the international prototype of the kilogram.
Light	Light is electromagnetic radiation with a wavelength that is visible to the eye (visible light) or, in a technical or scientific context, electromagnetic radiation of any wavelength.
Rate	A rate is a special kind of ratio, indicating a relationship between two measurements with different units, such as miles to gallons or cents to pounds.
Check	A check is a negotiable instrument instructing a financial institution to pay a specific amount of a specific currency from a specific demand account held in the maker/depositor face=symbol>¢s name with that institution. Both the maker and payee may be natural persons or legal entities.
Radius	In classical geometry, a radius of a circle or sphere is any line segment from its center to its boundary. By extension, the radius of a circle or sphere is the length of any such segment. The radius is half the diameter. In science and engineering the term radius of curvature is commonly used as a synonym for radius.
Diameter	In geometry, a diameter (Greek words diairo = divide and metro = measure) of a circle is any straight line segment that passes through the centre and whose endpoints are on the circular boundary, or, in more modern usage, the length of such a line segment. When using the word in the more modern sense, one speaks of the diameter rather than a diameter, because all diameters of a circle have the same length. This length is twice the radius. The diameter of a circle is also the longest chord that the circle has.
Square	In plane geometry, a square is a polygon with four equal sides, four right angles, and parallel opposite sides. In algebra, the square of a number is that number multiplied by itself.
Agriculture	Agriculture is the production of food, feed, fiber, fuel and other goods by the systematic raizing of plants and animals.
Mile	A mile is a unit of length, usually used to measure distance, in a number of different systems, including Imperial units, United States customary units and Norwegian/Swedish mil. Its size can vary from system to system, but in each is between 1 and 10 kilometers. In contemporary English contexts mile refers to either:
Travel	Travel is the transport of people on a trip/journey or the process or time involved in a person or object moving from one location to another.
Function	The mathematical concept of a function expresses the intuitive idea of deterministic dependence between two quantities, one of which is viewed as primary and the other as secondary. A function then is a way to associate a unique output for each input of a specified type, for example, a real number or an element of a given set.
Sequence	In mathematics, a sequence is an ordered list of objects. Like a set, it contains members, also called elements or terms, and the number of terms is called the length of the sequence. Unlike a set, order matters, and the exact same elements can appear multiple times at different positions in the sequence.
Column	In mathematics, a matrix can be thought of as each row or column being a vector. Hence, a space formed by row vectors or column vectors are said to be a row space or a column space.
Logarithm	In mathematics, a logarithm of a number x is the exponent y of the power by such that x = b^y. The value used for the base b must be neither 0 nor 1, nor a root of 1 in the case of the extension to complex numbers, and is typically 10, e, or 2.

Go to **Cram101.com** for the Practice Tests for this Chapter.

Period	In business, particularly accounting, a period is the time intervals that the accounts, statement, payments, or other calculations cover.
Minutes	Minutes are a measure of time.
Doubling time	The doubling time is the period of time required for a quantity to double in size or value.
Space	Space is a set, with some particular properties and usually some additional structure, such as the operations of addition or multiplication, for instance.
Napier	John Napier of Merchistoun , nicknamed Marvellous Merchistoun, was a Scottish mathematician, physicist, astronomer/astrologer and 8th Laird of Merchistoun. He is most remembered as the inventor of logarithms and Napier's bones, and for popularizing the use of the decimal point.
John Napier	John Napier of Nerchistoun, nicknamed Marvellous Merchistoun, was a Scottish mathematician, physicist, astronomer/astrologer and 8th Laird of Merchistoun.
Population	In sociology and biology a population is the collection of people or organisms of a particular species living in a given geographic area or space, usually measured by a census.
Pairs	In mathematics, the conjugate pairs or adjoint matrix of an m-by-n matrix A with complex entries is the n-by-m matrix A* obtained from A by taking the transpose and then taking the complex conjugate of each entry.
Scale	In Euclidean geometry, a uniform scale is a linear transformation that enlargers or diminishes objects, and whose scale factor is the same in all directions. This is also called homothethy.
Earthquake	An earthquake is the result from the sudden release of stored energy in the Earth face=symbol>¢s crust that creates seismic waves.
Magnitude	The magnitude of a mathematical object is its size: a property by which it can be larger or smaller than other objects of the same kind; in technical terms, an ordering of the class of objects to which it belongs.
Image	In mathematics, image is a part of the set theoretic notion of function.
Fractal	In colloquial usage, a fractal is "a rough or fragmented geometric shape that can be subdivided in parts, each of which is, at least approximately, a reduced-size copy of the whole."
Binary logarithm	In mathematics, the binary logarithm ,$\log_2 n$, is the logarithm for base 2. It is the inverse function of 2n.
Calculation	A calculation is a deliberate process for transforming one or more inputs into one or more results.
Astronomy	Astronomy is the scientific study of celestial objects such as stars, planets, comets, and galaxies; and phenomena that originate outside the Earth's atmosphere.
Decibel	The decibel relative to a specified or implied reference level.
Sound intensity	The sound intensity, i.e., acoustic intensity is defined as the sound power P_{ac} per unit area A.
Music	Multiple Signal Classification, also known as MUSIC, is an algorithm used for frequency estimation and emitter location.
Greater than	In mathematics, an inequality is a statement about the relative size or order of two objects. For example 14 > 10, or 14 is greater than 10.

33

Range	In mathematics, the range of a function is the set of all "output" values produced by that function. Given a function $f : A \rightarrow B$, the range of class="unicode">f, is defined to be the set {x class="unicode"> B:x= class="unicode">f(a) for some a class="unicode"> A}.
Leaves	In botany, leaves are above-ground plant organs specialized for photosynthesis. Their characteristics are typically analyzed by using Fiobonacci's sequences.
Diagram	A diagram is a simplified and structured visual representation of concepts, ideas, constructions, relations, statistical data, anatomy etc used in all aspects of human activities to visualize and clarify the topic.
Ruler	A ruler is an instrument used in geometry technical drawing and engineering/building to measure distances and/or to rule straight lines.
Interval	In elementary algebra, an interval is a set that contains every real number between two indicated numbers and may contain the two numbers themselves.
Turn	A turn is 360° or 2∂ radians.
Frequency	In statistics the frequency of an event i is the number n_i of times the event occurred in the experiment or the study. These frequencies are often graphically represented in histograms.
Amount	amount is a kind of property which exists as magnitude or multitude. It is among the basic classes of things along with quality, substance, change, and relation.
Exponential function	Exponential function is one of the most important functions in mathematics. A function commonly used to study growth and decay
Curve	In mathematics, the concept of a curve tries to capture the intuitive idea of a geometrical one-dimensional and continuous object. A simple example is the circle.
Axes	An axes is when two lines intersect somewhere on a plane creating a right angle at intersection
Measure	A measure is a function that assigns a number to subsets of a given set.
Units	The units of measurement are a globally standardized and modernized form of the metric system.
Element	An element or member of a set is an object that when collected together make up the set.
Statistics	Statistics is a mathematical science pertaining to the collection, analysis, interpretation or explanation, and presentation of data. It is applicable to a wide variety of academic disciplines, from the physical and social sciences to the humanities.
Experiment	In the scientific method, an experiment (Latin: ex-+-periri, "of (or from) trying"), is a set of actions and observations, performed in the context of solving a particular problem or question, in order to support or falsify a hypothesis or research concerning phenomena.
Axis	An axis is a straight line around which a geometric figure can be rotated.
Average	In mathematics, an average, mean, or central tendency of a data set refers to a measure of the "middle" or "expected" value of the data set.
Test	Acid test ratio measures the ability of a company to use its near cash or quick assets to immediately extinguish its current liabilities.

Go to **Cram101.com** for the Practice Tests for this Chapter.

Variable	A variable is a symbolic representation denoting a quantity or expression. It often represents an "unknown" quantity that has the potential to change.
Meter	The metre (or meter, see spelling differences) is a measure of length. It is the basic unit of length in the metric system and in the International System of Units (SI), used around the world for general and scientific purposes.
Counting	Counting is the mathematical action of repeatedly adding or subtracting one, usually to find out how many objects there are or to set aside a desired number of objects.
Number system	number system is a set of numbers, in the broadest sense of the word, together with one or more operations, such as addition or multiplication.
Universal	Universal algebra (sometimes called General algebra) is the field of mathematics that studies the ideas common to all algebraic structures.
Planet	A planet, as defined by the International Astronomical Union , is a celestial body orbiting a star or stellar remnant that is massive enough to be rounded by its own gravity, not massive enough to cause thermonuclear fusion in its core, and has cleared its neighboring region of planetesimals.
Geometric sequence	A geometric sequence is a sequence of numbers where each term after the first is found by multiplying the previous one by a fixed non-zero number called the common ratio.
Volume	The volume of a solid object is the three-dimensional concept of how much space it occupies, often quantified numerically.
Slide	The slide rule, also known as a slipstick, is a mechanical analog computer, consisting of at least two finely divided scales , most often a fixed outer pair and a movable inner one, with a sliding window called the cursor.
Classes	In set theory and its applications throughout mathematics, classes are a collection of sets (or sometimes other mathematical objects) that can be unambiguously defined by a property that all its members share.

Go to **Cram101.com** for the Practice Tests for this Chapter.

Regular	In mathematics, a regular function in the sense of algebraic geometry is an everywhere-defined, polynomial function on an algebraic variety V with values in the field K over which V is defined.
Symmetry	Symmetry means "constancy", i.e. if something retains a certain feature even after we change a way of looking at it, then it is symmetric.
Center	In geometry, the center of an object is a point in some sense in the middle of the object.
Reflection	In mathematics, a reflection (also spelled reflexion) is a map that transforms an object into its mirror image.
Perpendicular	In geometry, two lines or planes if one falls on the other in such a way as to create congruent adjacent angles. The term may be used as a noun or adjective. Thus, referring to Figure 1, the line AB is the perpendicular to CD through the point B.
Horizontal	In astronomy, geography, geometry and related sciences and contexts, a plane is said to be horizontal at a given point if it is locally perpendicular to the gradient of the gravity field, i.e., with the direction of the gravitational force at that point.
Square	In plane geometry, a square is a polygon with four equal sides, four right angles, and parallel opposite sides. In algebra, the square of a number is that number multiplied by itself.
Opposite	In mathematics, the additive inverse, or opposite of a number n is the number that, when added to n, yields zero. The additive inverse of n is denoted −n. For example, 7 is −7, because 7 + (−7) = 0, and the additive inverse of −0.3 is 0.3, because −0.3 + 0.3 = 0.
Additive inverse	In mathematics, the additive inverse of a number n is the number that, when added to n, yields zero. The additive inverse of n is denoted −n. For example, 7 is −7, because 7 + (−7) = 0, and the additive inverse of −0.3 is 0.3, because −0.3 + 0.3 = 0.
Axis	An axis is a straight line around which a geometric figure can be rotated.
Axis of symmetry	Axis of symmetry of a two-dimensional figure is a line such that, if a perpendicular is constructed, any two points lying on the perpendicular at equal distances from the axis of symmetry are identical.
Turn	A turn is 360° or 2δ radians.
Rotational	In linear algebra and geometry, a rotation (rotational) is a type of transformation from one system of coordinates to another system of coordinates such that distance between any two points remains invariant under the transformation.
Trace	In linear algebra, the trace of an n-by-n square matrix A is defined to be the sum of the elements on the main diagonal of A,
Star	In star algebra, a *-ring is an associative ring with an antilinear, antiautomorphism * : A ¨ A which is an involution.
Mean	The mean, the average in everyday English, which is also called the arithmetic mean (and is distinguished from the geometric mean or harmonic mean). The average is also called the sample mean. The expected value of a random variable, which is also called the population mean.
Triangle	A triangle is one of the basic shapes of geometry: a polygon with three vertices and three sides which are straight line segments.
Equilateral	In geometry, an equilateral polygon is a polygon which has all sides of the same length.
Equilateral triangle	An Equilateral Triangle is a triangle in which all sides are of equal length.

Go to **Cram101.com** for the Practice Tests for this Chapter.

Polygon	In geometry a polygon is a plane figure that is bounded by a closed path or circuit, composed of a finite number of sequential line segments.
Polygons	In geometry, polygons are plane figures that are bounded by a closed path or circuit, composed of a finite number of sequential line segments.
Counting	Counting is the mathematical action of repeatedly adding or subtracting one, usually to find out how many objects there are or to set aside a desired number of objects.
Circle	In Euclidean geometry, a circle is the set of all points in a plane at a fixed distance, called the radius, from a given point, the center.
Enneagon	An enneagon is a nine-sided polygon.
Image	In mathematics, image is a part of the set theoretic notion of function.
Measure	A measure is a function that assigns a number to subsets of a given set.
Pentagon	In geometry, a pentagon is any five-sided polygon.
Degree	In mathematics, there are several meanings of degree depending on the subject.
Sum	A sum is the result of the addition of a set of numbers. The numbers may be natural numbers, complex numbers, matrices, or still more complicated objects. An infinite sum is a subtle procedure known as a series.
Arc	In Euclidean geometry, an arc is a closed segment of a differentiable curve in the two-dimensional plane; for example, a circular arc is a segment of a circle.
Straightedge	A straightedge is a tool similar to a ruler, but without markings.
Intersecting	In geometry, intersecting lines are two lines that share one or more common points.
Hexagon	A hexagon is a polygon with six edges and six vertices.
Interest	Interest is the fee paid on borrowed money.
Construction	Compass and straightedge or ruler-and-compass construction is the construction of lengths or angles using only an idealized ruler and compass.
Radius	In classical geometry, a radius of a circle or sphere is any line segment from its center to its boundary. By extension, the radius of a circle or sphere is the length of any such segment. The radius is half the diameter. In science and engineering the term radius of curvature is commonly used as a synonym for radius.
Protractor	In geometry, protractor is a circular or semicircular tool for measuring angles. The units of measurement utilized are usually degrees.
Drawings	Drawings (i.e. Plans) are a set of two-dimensional diagrams or drawings used to describe a place or object, or to communicate building or fabrication instructions.
Segment	In geometry, a line segment is a part of a line that is bounded by two end points, and contains every point on the line between its end points.
Line segment	A line segment is a part of a line that is bounded by two end points, and contains every point on the line between its end points.
Ruler	A ruler is an instrument used in geometry technical drawing and engineering/building to measure distances and/or to rule straight lines.
Octagon	An octagon is a polygon that has eight sides.
Space	Space is a set, with some particular properties and usually some additional structure, such as the operations of addition or multiplication, for instance.

Semiregular   A polyhedron or plane tessellation is called semiregular when its faces are all regular polyhedrons and its corners are alike. Another name for a semiregular polyhedron is an Archimedean Solid.

Light   Light is electromagnetic radiation with a wavelength that is visible to the eye (visible light) or, in a technical or scientific context, electromagnetic radiation of any wavelength.

Combination   In combinatorial mathematics, a combination is an un-ordered collection of unique elements.

Shapes   Shapes are external two-dimensional outlines, with the appearance or configuration of some thing - in contrast to the matter or content or substance of which it is composed.

Symbols   Symbols are objects, characters, or other concrete representations of ideas, concepts, or other abstractions.

Repeating   A repeating decimal is a number whose decimal representation eventually becomes periodic (i.e. the same number sequence repeating indefinitely).

Kite   In geometry a kite, or deltoid, is a quadrilateral with two pairs of congruent adjacent sides.

Diagram   A diagram is a simplified and structured visual representation of concepts, ideas, constructions, relations, statistical data, anatomy etc used in all aspects of human activities to visualize and clarify the topic.

Polyhedron   A polyhedron (plural polyhedra or polyhedrons) is a geometric object with flat faces and straight edges.

Solid   In mathematics, solid geometry was the traditional name for the geometry of three-dimensional Euclidean space — for practical purposes the kind of space we live in.

Tetrahedron   A tetrahedron (plural: tetrahedra) is a polyhedron composed of four triangular faces, three of which meet at each vertex.

Octahedron   An octahedron is a polyhedron with eight faces.

Icosahedron   An icosahedronis any polyhedron having 20 faces, but usually a regular icosahedron is implied, which has equilateral triangles as faces.

Cube   A cube is a three-dimensional solid object bounded by six square faces, facets, or sides, with three meeting at each vertex.

Gap   GAP (Groups, Algorithms and Programming) is a computer algebra system for computational discrete algebra with particular emphasis on, but not restricted to, computational group theory.

Dodecahedron   A dodecahedron is any polyhedron with twelve faces, but usually a regular dodecahedron is meant: a Platonic solid composed of twelve regular pentagonal faces, with three meeting at each vertex.

Pythagoras   Pythagoras was an Greek philosopher. He is best known for a theorem in trigonometry that bears his name.

Regular polyhedra   Regular polyhedra are polyhedra whose faces are identical (or, technically, congruent) regular polygons and which have the same number of faces around each vertex.

Plato   Plato whose original name was Aristocles, was an ancient Greek philosopher, the second of the great trio of ancient Greeks –succeeding Socrates and preceeding Aristotle– who between them laid the philosophical foundations of Western culture.

Polyhedra   Polyhedra are geometric objects with flat faces and straight edges.

Element   An element or member of a set is an object that when collected together make up the set.

Go to **Cram101.com** for the Practice Tests for this Chapter.

Elements	In mathematics, the elements ﹐ or members of a set or more generally a class are all those objects which when collected together make up the set or class.
Cubes	Cubes are of a number n in its third power-the result of multiplying it by itself three times.
Universe	The Universe is defined as the summation of all particles and energy that exist and the space-time which all events occur.
Pyramid	An n-sided pyramid is a polyhedron formed by connecting an n-sided polygonal base and a point, called the apex, by n triangular faces. In other words, it is a conic solid with polygonal base.
Ring	In mathematics, a ring is an algebraic structure in which addition and multiplication are defined and have properties listed below.
Lewis Carroll	Lewis Carroll was an English author, mathematician, logician, Anglican clergyman and photographer.
Archimedean solid	In geometry an Archimedean solid is a highly symmetric, semi-regular convex polyhedron composed of two or more types of regular polygons meeting in identical vertices.
Archimedes	Archimedes of Syracuse was an ancient Greek mathematician, physicist and engineer. In addition to making important discoveries in the field of mathematics and geometry, he is credited with producing machines that were well ahead of their time.
Sphere	In mathematics, a sphere is the set of all points in three-dimensional space (R^3) which are at distance r from a fixed point of that space, where r is a positive real number called the radius of the sphere. The fixed point is called the center or centre, and is not part of the sphere itself.
Vertex	In geometry, a vertex is a special kind of point, usually a corner of a polygon, polyhedron, or higher dimensional polytope. In the geometry of curves a vertex is a point of where the first derivative of curvature is zero. In graph theory, a vertex is the fundamental unit out of which graphs are formed
Bond	Bond finance, in finance, a debt security, issued by Issuer
Prisms	In geometry, n-sided prisms are polyhedra made of an n-sided polygonal base, a translated copy, and n faces joining corresponding sides.
Of the world	The population of the world is the total number of human beings alive on the planet Earth at a given time.
Isosceles	An Isosceles triange is a triangle with at least two sides of equal length.
Rectangle	In geometry, a rectangle is defined as a quadrilateral where all four of its angles are right angles.
Range	In mathematics, the range of a function is the set of all "output" values produced by that function. Given a function f :A $\rightarrow$ B, the range of class="unicode">f, is defined to be the set {x class="unicode"> B:x= class="unicode">f(a) for some a class="unicode"> A}.
Column	In mathematics, a matrix can be thought of as each row or column being a vector. Hence, a space formed by row vectors or column vectors are said to be a row space or a column space.
Spectrum	A spectrum is a condition or value that is not limited to a specific set of values but can

vary infinitely within a continuum.

Series

A series is the sum of the elements of a sequence.

Overhead

In business, overhead, overhead cost or overhead expense refers to an ongoing expense of operating a business.

Euler

Leonhard Euler was a pioneering Swiss mathematician and physicist, who spent most of his life in Russia and Germany.

Expression

An expression is a combination of numbers, operators, grouping symbols and/or free variables and bound variables arranged in a meaningful way which can be evaluated..

Decagon

In geometry, a decagon is any polygon with ten sides and ten angles, and usually refers to a regular decagon, having all sides of equal length and all angles equal to 144¡ã, therefore making each angle of a regular decagon be 144¡ã.

Heptagon

A heptagon is a polygon with seven sides and seven angles.

Knot

A knot is a method for fastening or securing linear material such as rope by tying or interweaving. It may consist of a length of one or more segments of rope, string, webbing, twine, strap or even chain interwoven so as to create in the line the ability to bind to itself or to some other object - the "load". Knots have been the subject of interest both for their ancient origins, common use, and the mathematical implications of knot theory.

Planet

A planet, as defined by the International Astronomical Union , is a celestial body orbiting a star or stellar remnant that is massive enough to be rounded by its own gravity, not massive enough to cause thermonuclear fusion in its core, and has cleared its neighboring region of planetesimals.

Tension

Tension is a reaction force applied by a stretched string on the objects which stretch it.

Frequency

In statistics the frequency of an event i is the number n_i of times the event occurred in the experiment or the study. These frequencies are often graphically represented in histograms.

Omega

Omega (uppercase Î©, lowercase Ï‰) In the Greek numeric system it has a value of 800. The word literally means "great O" (Å   mega, mega meaning ′great face=symbol>¢), as opposed to Omicron, which means "little O" (o mikron, micron meaning "little").[1] This name is Byzantine; in Classical Greek, the letter was called Å (á½¦), whereas the Omicron was called ou (Î¿á½–).[2] The form of the letter derives from a double omicron, which came to be written open at the top.

Minus

The plus and minus signs are mathematical symbols used to represent the notions of positive and negative as well as the operations of addition and subtraction.

Prediction

A prediction is a statement or claimt that a particular event will occur in the future in more certain terms than a forecast.

Coordinate

A coordinate is a set of numbers that designate location in a given reference system, such as x,y in a planar coordinate system or an x,y,z in a three-dimensional coordinate system.

Ptolemy

Claudius Ptolemaeus, known in English as Ptolemy, was a Hellenistic mathematician, geographer, astronomer, and astrologer. The Almagest is widely held to be the first systematic treatise on astronomy in antiquity. Babylonian astronomers had developed arithmetical techniques for calculating astronomical phenomena; Greek astronomers such as Hipparchus had produced geometric models for calculating celestial motions; Ptolemy, however, clearly derived his geometrical models from selected astronomical observations by his predecessors spanning more than 800 years.

Plane

In mathematics, a plane is a two-dimensional manifold or surface that is perfectly flat.

Rigid	In mathematics, suppose C is a collection of mathematical objects . Then we say that C is rigid if every c $\in$ C is uniquely determined by less information about c than one would expect.
Architecture	Architecture is the art and science of designing buildings and structures.
Descartes	Descartes was a highly influential French philosopher, mathematician, scientist, and writer. Dubbed the "Founder of Modern Philosophy", and the "Father of Modern Mathematics". His theories provided the basis for the calculus of Newton and Leibniz, by applying infinitesimal calculus to the tangent line problem, thus permitting the evolution of that branch of modern mathematics
Angular	In physics, the angular momentum of an object rotating about some reference point is the measure of the extent to which the object will continue to rotate about that point unless acted upon by an external torque.
Proof	In mathematics, a proof is a demonstration that, assuming certain axioms, some statement is necessarily true.

Go to **Cram101.com** for the Practice Tests for this Chapter.

Circle	In Euclidean geometry, a circle is the set of all points in a plane at a fixed distance, called the radius, from a given point, the center.
Ellipse	In mathematics, an ellipse .
Curve	In mathematics, the concept of a curve tries to capture the intuitive idea of a geometrical one-dimensional and continuous object. A simple example is the circle.
Curves	In mathematics, curves are the intuitive idea of a geometrical one-dimensional and continuous object.
Orbit	In physics, an orbit is the path that an object makes around another object while under the influence of a source of centripetal force, such as gravity.
Satellites	In the context of spaceflight, a satellites are any object which has been placed into orbit by human endeavor.
Communications	Communications are procedures that allow people to exchange information by one of several methods.
Plane	In mathematics, a plane is a two-dimensional manifold or surface that is perfectly flat.
Center	In geometry, the center of an object is a point in some sense in the middle of the object.
Radius	In classical geometry, a radius of a circle or sphere is any line segment from its center to its boundary. By extension, the radius of a circle or sphere is the length of any such segment. The radius is half the diameter. In science and engineering the term radius of curvature is commonly used as a synonym for radius.
Sum	A sum is the result of the addition of a set of numbers. The numbers may be natural numbers, complex numbers, matrices, or still more complicated objects. An infinite sum is a subtle procedure known as a series.
Shapes	Shapes are external two-dimensional outlines, with the appearance or configuration of some thing - in contrast to the matter or content or substance of which it is composed.
Axis	An axis is a straight line around which a geometric figure can be rotated.
Minor	In linear algebra, a minor of a matrix A is the determinant of some smaller square matrix, cut down from A.
Apollonius	Apollonius of Perga was a Greek geometer and astronomer, of the Alexandrian school, noted for his writings on conic sections. His innovative methodology and terminology, especially in the field of conics, influenced many later scholars including Ptolemy, Francesco Maurolico, Isaac Newton, and René Descartes. It was Apollonius who gave the ellipse, the parabola, and the hyperbola the names by which we know them. The hypothesis of eccentric orbits, or equivalently, deferent and epicycles, to explain the apparent motion of the planets and the varying speed of the Moon, are also attributed to him.
Planet	A planet, as defined by the International Astronomical Union , is a celestial body orbiting a star or stellar remnant that is massive enough to be rounded by its own gravity, not massive enough to cause thermonuclear fusion in its core, and has cleared its neighboring region of planetesimals.
Turn	A turn is 360° or 2δ radians.
Units	The units of measurement are a globally standardized and modernized form of the metric system.
Axes	An axes is when two lines intersect somewhere on a plane creating a right angle at intersection

Go to **Cram101.com** for the Practice Tests for this Chapter.

Origin	In mathematics, the origin of a coordinate system is the point where the axes of the system intersect.
Experiment	In the scientific method, an experiment (Latin: ex-+-periri, "of (or from) trying"), is a set of actions and observations, performed in the context of solving a particular problem or question, in order to support or falsify a hypothesis or research concerning phenomena.
Perpendicular	In geometry, two lines or planes if one falls on the other in such a way as to create congruent adjacent angles. The term may be used as a noun or adjective. Thus, referring to Figure 1, the line AB is the perpendicular to CD through the point B.
Foci	In geometry, the foci are a pair of special points used in describing conic sections. The four types of conic sections are the circle, parabola, ellipse, and hyperbola.
Newton	Sir Isaac Newton, was an English physicist, mathematician, astronomer, natural philosopher, and alchemist, regarded by many as the greatest figure in the history of science
Trace	In linear algebra, the trace of an n-by-n square matrix A is defined to be the sum of the elements on the main diagonal of A,
Parabola	In mathematics, the parabola is a conic section generated by the intersection of a right circular conical surface and a plane parallel to a generating straight line of that surface. It can also be defined as locus of points in a plane which are equidistant from a given point.
Space	Space is a set, with some particular properties and usually some additional structure, such as the operations of addition or multiplication, for instance.
Galileo Galilei	Galileo Galilei was an Italian physicist, mathematician, astronomer, and philosopher who is closely associated with the scientific revolution.
Symmetry	Symmetry means "constancy", i.e. if something retains a certain feature even after we change a way of looking at it, then it is symmetric.
Paraboloid	Paraboloid is a quadric
Rays	In geometry and physics, rays are half-lines that continue forever in one direction.
Light	Light is electromagnetic radiation with a wavelength that is visible to the eye (visible light) or, in a technical or scientific context, electromagnetic radiation of any wavelength.
Scale	In Euclidean geometry, a uniform scale is a linear transformation that enlargers or diminishes objects, and whose scale factor is the same in all directions. This is also called homothethy.
Measure	A measure is a function that assigns a number to subsets of a given set.
Hyperbola	In mathematics, a hyperbola is a type of conic section defined as the intersection between a right circular conical surface and a plane which cuts through both halves of the cone.
Cone	A cone is a three-dimensional geometric shape formed by straight lines through a fixed point (vertex) to the points of a fixed curve (directrix)
Horizontal	In astronomy, geography, geometry and related sciences and contexts, a plane is said to be horizontal at a given point if it is locally perpendicular to the gradient of the gravity field, i.e., with the direction of the gravitational force at that point.
Conic	In mathematics, a conic section is a curve that can be formed by intersecting a cone with a plane.
Travel	Travel is the transport of people on a trip/journey or the process or time involved in a person or object moving from one location to another.

Go to **Cram101.com** for the Practice Tests for this Chapter.

Check	A check is a negotiable instrument instructing a financial institution to pay a specific amount of a specific currency from a specific demand account held in the maker/depositor face=symbol>¢s name with that institution. Both the maker and payee may be natural persons or legal entities.
Ruler	A ruler is an instrument used in geometry technical drawing and engineering/building to measure distances and/or to rule straight lines.
Graphs	Graphs are the basic objects of study in graph theory. Informally speaking, a graph is a set of objects called points, nodes, or vertices connected by links called lines or edges.
Asymptote	An asymptote is a straight line or curve A to which another curve B approaches closer and closer as one moves along it. As one moves along B, the space between it and the asymptote A becomes smaller and smaller, and can in fact be made as small as one could wish by going far enough along. A curve may or may not touch or cross its asymptote. In fact, the curve may intersect the asymptote an infinite number of times.
Coordinate	A coordinate is a set of numbers that designate location in a given reference system, such as x,y in a planar coordinate system or an x,y,z in a three-dimensional coordinate system.
Rectangle	In geometry, a rectangle is defined as a quadrilateral where all four of its angles are right angles.
Sine	Sine is a trigonemtric function that is important when studying triangles and modeling periodic phenomena, among other applications.
Function	The mathematical concept of a function expresses the intuitive idea of deterministic dependence between two quantities, one of which is viewed as primary and the other as secondary. A function then is a way to associate a unique output for each input of a specified type, for example, a real number or an element of a given set.
Period	In business, particularly accounting, a period is the time intervals that the accounts, statement, payments, or other calculations cover.
Rate	A rate is a special kind of ratio, indicating a relationship between two measurements with different units, such as miles to gallons or cents to pounds.
Latitude	Latitude, usually denoted symbolically by the Greek letter phi, class=Unicode>Î¦, gives the location of a place on Earth north or south of the equator. Latitude is an angular measurement in degrees (marked with Â°) ranging from 0Â° at the Equator (low latitude) to 90Â° at the poles (90Â° N for the North Pole or 90Â° S for the South Pole; high latitude). The complementary angle of a latitude is called the colatitude.
Amplitude	The amplitude is a nonnegative scalar measure of a wave's magnitude of oscillation, that is, the magnitude of the maximum disturbance in the medium during one wave cycle.
Regular	In mathematics, a regular function in the sense of algebraic geometry is an everywhere-defined, polynomial function on an algebraic variety V with values in the field K over which V is defined.
Sound wave	Sound is a disturbance of mechanical energy that propagates through matter as a wave or sound wave.
Image	In mathematics, image is a part of the set theoretic notion of function.
Tuning fork	A tuning fork is a simple metal two-pronged fork with the tines formed from a U-shaped bar of elastic material .
Frequency	In statistics the frequency of an event i is the number n_i of times the event occurred in the experiment or the study. These frequencies are often graphically represented

Go to **Cram101.com** for the Practice Tests for this Chapter.

in histograms.

Series	A series is the sum of the elements of a sequence.
Compact	In mathematics, a subset of Euclidean space R^n is called compact if it is closed and bounded.
Spirals	In mathematics, a spirals are a curve which emanates from a central point, getting progressively farther away as it revolves around the point.
Archimedes	Archimedes of Syracuse was an ancient Greek mathematician, physicist and engineer. In addition to making important discoveries in the field of mathematics and geometry, he is credited with producing machines that were well ahead of their time.
Interval	In elementary algebra, an interval is a set that contains every real number between two indicated numbers and may contain the two numbers themselves.
Analytic geometry	Analytic geometry is the study of geometry using the principles of algebra. Analytic geometry can be explained more simply: it is concerned with defining geometrical shapes in a numerical way and extracting numerical information from that representation.
Descartes	Descartes was a highly influential French philosopher, mathematician, scientist, and writer. Dubbed the "Founder of Modern Philosophy", and the "Father of Modern Mathematics". His theories provided the basis for the calculus of Newton and Leibniz, by applying infinitesimal calculus to the tangent line problem, thus permitting the evolution of that branch of modern mathematics
Sequence	In mathematics, a sequence is an ordered list of objects. Like a set, it contains members, also called elements or terms, and the number of terms is called the length of the sequence. Unlike a set, order matters, and the exact same elements can appear multiple times at different positions in the sequence.
Geometric sequence	A geometric sequence is a sequence of numbers where each term after the first is found by multiplying the previous one by a fixed non-zero number called the common ratio.
Universe	The Universe is defined as the summation of all particles and energy that exist and the space-time which all events occur.
Star	In star algebra, a *-ring is an associative ring with an antilinear, antiautomorphism * : A ¨ A which is an involution.
Photography	Photography is the process of recording pictures by means of capturing light on a light-sensitive medium, such as a film or sensor.
Arithmetic	Arithmetic or arithmetics is the oldest and most elementary branch of mathematics, used by almost everyone, for tasks ranging from simple daily counting to advanced science and business calculations.
Arithmetic sequence	Arithmetic sequence is a sequence of numbers such that the difference of any two successive members of the sequence is a constant.
Cycloid	A cycloid is the curve defined by the path of a point on the edge of circular wheel as the wheel rolls along a straight line.
Arc	In Euclidean geometry, an arc is a closed segment of a differentiable curve in the two-dimensional plane; for example, a circular arc is a segment of a circle.
Epicycloid	Epicycloid is a plane curve produced by tracing the path of a chosen point of a circle — called epicycle — which rolls without slipping around a fixed circle. It is a particular kind of roulette.
Hypocycloids	In geometry, a hypocycloids are a special plane curve generated by the trace of a fixed point

Go to **Cram101.com** for the Practice Tests for this Chapter.

on a small circle that rolls within a larger circle.

Circumference	The circumference is the distance around a closed curve. Circumference is a kind of perimeter.
Diameter	In geometry, a diameter (Greek words diairo = divide and metro = measure) of a circle is any straight line segment that passes through the centre and whose endpoints are on the circular boundary, or, in more modern usage, the length of such a line segment. When using the word in the more modern sense, one speaks of the diameter rather than a diameter, because all diameters of a circle have the same length. This length is twice the radius. The diameter of a circle is also the longest chord that the circle has.
Protractor	In geometry, protractor is a circular or semicircular tool for measuring angles. The units of measurement utilized are usually degrees.
Cardioid	In geometry, the cardioid is an epicycloid with one cusp. That is, a cardioid is a curve that can be produced as the path of a point on the circumference of a circle as that circle rolls around another fixed circle with the same radius.
Constant	In mathematics and the mathematical sciences, a constant is a fixed, but possibly unspecified, value. This is in contrast to a variable, which is not fixed.
Solid	In mathematics, solid geometry was the traditional name for the geometry of three-dimensional Euclidean space — for practical purposes the kind of space we live in.
Voltage	Voltage is the difference of electrical potential between two points of an electrical or electronic circuit, expressed in volts
Whispering gallery	A whispering gallery is a gallery beneath a dome or vault or enclosed in a circular or elliptical area in which whispers can be heard clearly in other parts of the building.
Sir Christopher Wren	Sir Christopher Wren was a 17th century English designer, astronomer, geometer, and one of the greatest English architects of his time. Wren designed 53 London churches, including St Paul's Cathedral, as well as many secular buildings of note. He was a founder of the Royal Society, and his scientific work was highly regarded by Sir Isaac Newton and Blaise Pascal.
Endpoint	In geometry, an endpoint is a point at which a line segment or ray terminates.
Parallel lines	The existence and properties of parallel lines are the basis of Euclid face=symbol>¢s parallel postulate. Parallel lines are two lines on the same plane that do not intersect even assuming that lines extend to infinity in either direction.
Consecutive	Consecutive means in succession or back-to-back
Intersection	In mathematics, the intersection of two sets A and B is the set that contains all elements of A that also belong to B (or equivalently, all elements of B that also belong to A), but no other elements.
Opposite	In mathematics, the additive inverse, or opposite of a number n is the number that, when added to n, yields zero. The additive inverse of n is denoted −n. For example, 7 is −7, because 7 + (−7) = 0, and the additive inverse of −0.3 is 0.3, because −0.3 + 0.3 = 0.
Additive inverse	In mathematics, the additive inverse of a number n is the number that, when added to n, yields zero. The additive inverse of n is denoted −n. For example, 7 is −7, because 7 + (−7) = 0, and the additive inverse of −0.3 is 0.3, because −0.3 + 0.3 = 0.

Diagram	A diagram is a simplified and structured visual representation of concepts, ideas, constructions, relations, statistical data, anatomy etc used in all aspects of human activities to visualize and clarify the topic.
Feature	In geographic information systems, a feature comprises an entity with a geographic location, typically determined by points, arcs, or polygons. Carriageways and cadastres exemplify feature data.
Balance	In banking and accountancy, the outstanding balance is the amount of money owned, or due, that remains in a deposit account or a loan account at a given date, after all past remittances, payments and withdrawal have been accounted for.
Sequence	In mathematics, a sequence is an ordered list of objects. Like a set, it contains members, also called elements or terms, and the number of terms is called the length of the sequence. Unlike a set, order matters, and the exact same elements can appear multiple times at different positions in the sequence.
Principle	A principle signifies a point or points of probability on a subject e.g., the principle of creativity, which allows for the formation of rule or norm or law by interpretation of the phenomena events that can be created.
Counting	Counting is the mathematical action of repeatedly adding or subtracting one, usually to find out how many objects there are or to set aside a desired number of objects.
Fundamental Counting Principle	The Fundamental Counting Principle is a method that is used to calculate all of the possibilities of a pertaining number of events.
Shapes	Shapes are external two-dimensional outlines, with the appearance or configuration of some thing - in contrast to the matter or content or substance of which it is composed.
Bar	The bar (symbol bar) and the millibar (symbol mbar, also mb) are units of pressure.
Code	In mathematical logic, a Gödel numbering (or Gödel code) is a function that assigns to each symbol and well-formed formula of some formal language a unique natural number called its Gödel number.
Horizontal	In astronomy, geography, geometry and related sciences and contexts, a plane is said to be horizontal at a given point if it is locally perpendicular to the gradient of the gravity field, i.e., with the direction of the gravitational force at that point.
Permutation	Permutation is the rearrangement of objects or symbols into distinguishable sequences.
Factorial	Factorial of a non-negative integer n is the product of all positive integers less than or equal to n.
Center	In geometry, the center of an object is a point in some sense in the middle of the object.
Combination	In combinatorial mathematics, a combination is an un-ordered collection of unique elements.
Equivalent	Equivalence is the condition of being equivalent or essentially equal.
Expression	An expression is a combination of numbers, operators, grouping symbols and/or free variables and bound variables arranged in a meaningful way which can be evaluated..
Check	A check is a negotiable instrument instructing a financial institution to pay a specific amount of a specific currency from a specific demand account held in the maker/depositor face=symbol>¢s name with that institution. Both the maker and payee may be natural persons or legal entities.
Turn	A turn is 360° or 2δ radians.

Go to **Cram101.com** for the Practice Tests for this Chapter.

Consecutive	Consecutive means in succession or back-to-back
Pairs	In mathematics, the conjugate pairs or adjoint matrix of an m-by-n matrix A with complex entries is the n-by-m matrix A* obtained from A by taking the transpose and then taking the complex conjugate of each entry.
Product	In mathematics, a product is the result of multiplying, or an expression that identifies factors to be multiplied.
Circle	In Euclidean geometry, a circle is the set of all points in a plane at a fixed distance, called the radius, from a given point, the center.
Solid	In mathematics, solid geometry was the traditional name for the geometry of three-dimensional Euclidean space — for practical purposes the kind of space we live in.
Events	In probability theory, events are various sets of outcomes (a subset of the sample space) to which a probability is assigned.
Conjunction	In logic and mathematics, logical conjunction (usual symbol and) is a two-place logical operation that results in a value of true if both of its operands are true, otherwise a value of false.
Translation	In Euclidean geometry, a translation is moving every point a constant distance in a specified direction.
Rate	A rate is a special kind of ratio, indicating a relationship between two measurements with different units, such as miles to gallons or cents to pounds.
Ring	In mathematics, a ring is an algebraic structure in which addition and multiplication are defined and have properties listed below.
Series	A series is the sum of the elements of a sequence.
Square	In plane geometry, a square is a polygon with four equal sides, four right angles, and parallel opposite sides. In algebra, the square of a number is that number multiplied by itself.

Probability	Probability is the chance that something is likely to happen or be the case.
Gerolamo Cardano	Gerolamo Cardano or Girolamo Cardano was a celebrated Italian Renaissance mathematician, physician, astrologer, and gambler.
Scale	In Euclidean geometry, a uniform scale is a linear transformation that enlargers or diminishes objects, and whose scale factor is the same in all directions. This is also called homothethy.
Ratio	A ratio is a quantity that denotes the proportional amount or magnitude of one quantity relative to another.
Events	In probability theory, events are various sets of outcomes (a subset of the sample space) to which a probability is assigned.
Equally likely	If the probabilities of simple events are all the same, then they are equally likely. This occurs in a uniform sample space.
Turn	A turn is 360° or 2δ radians.
Multiple	A multiple of a number is the product of that number with any integer.
Measure	A measure is a function that assigns a number to subsets of a given set.
Test	Acid test ratio measures the ability of a company to use its near cash or quick assets to immediately extinguish its current liabilities.
Opposite	In mathematics, the additive inverse, or opposite of a number n is the number that, when added to n, yields zero. The additive inverse of n is denoted −n. For example, 7 is −7, because 7 + (−7) = 0, and the additive inverse of −0.3 is 0.3, because −0.3 + 0.3 = 0.
Additive inverse	In mathematics, the additive inverse of a number n is the number that, when added to n, yields zero. The additive inverse of n is denoted −n. For example, 7 is −7, because 7 + (−7) = 0, and the additive inverse of −0.3 is 0.3, because −0.3 + 0.3 = 0.
Column	In mathematics, a matrix can be thought of as each row or column being a vector. Hence, a space formed by row vectors or column vectors are said to be a row space or a column space.
Sector	A circular sector or circle sector also known as a pie piece is the portion of a circle enclosed by two radii and an arc.
Triple	In mathematics, a triple is an n-tuple with n being 3.
Ring	In mathematics, a ring is an algebraic structure in which addition and multiplication are defined and have properties listed below.
Percent	percent is a way of expressing a number as a fraction of 100 per cent meaning "per hundred".
Sum	A sum is the result of the addition of a set of numbers. The numbers may be natural numbers, complex numbers, matrices, or still more complicated objects. An infinite sum is a subtle procedure known as a series.
Counting	Counting is the mathematical action of repeatedly adding or subtracting one, usually to find out how many objects there are or to set aside a desired number of objects.
Galileo Galilei	Galileo Galilei was an Italian physicist, mathematician, astronomer, and philosopher who is closely associated with the scientific revolution.
Combination	In combinatorial mathematics, a combination is an un-ordered collection of unique elements.
Permutation	Permutation is the rearrangement of objects or symbols into distinguishable sequences.
Consecutive	Consecutive means in succession or back-to-back

Go to **Cram101.com** for the Practice Tests for this Chapter.

Plane	In mathematics, a plane is a two-dimensional manifold or surface that is perfectly flat.
Planes	In mathematics, planes are two-dimensional manifolds or surfaces that are perfectly flat.
Space	Space is a set, with some particular properties and usually some additional structure, such as the operations of addition or multiplication, for instance.
Diagram	A diagram is a simplified and structured visual representation of concepts, ideas, constructions, relations, statistical data, anatomy etc used in all aspects of human activities to visualize and clarify the topic.
Binomial	In elementary algebra, a binomial is a polynomial with two terms: the sum of two monomials. It is the simplest kind of polynomial except for a monomial.
Binomial probability	Binomial probability typically deals with the probability of several successive decisions, each of which has two possible outcomes.
Whole number	In mathematics, a whole number can mean either an element of the set {1, 2, 3, ...} (i.e the positive integers) or an element of the set {0, 1, 2, 3, ...} (i.e. the non-negative integers).
Experiment	In the scientific method, an experiment (Latin: ex-+-periri, "of (or from) trying"), is a set of actions and observations, performed in the context of solving a particular problem or question, in order to support or falsify a hypothesis or research concerning phenomena.
Intersection	In mathematics, the intersection of two sets A and B is the set that contains all elements of A that also belong to B (or equivalently, all elements of B that also belong to A), but no other elements.
Triangle	A triangle is one of the basic shapes of geometry: a polygon with three vertices and three sides which are straight line segments.
Pascal	Blaise Pascal was a French mathematician, physicist, and religious philosopher.
Blaise Pascal	Blaise Pascal was a French mathematician, physicist, and religious philosopher.
Birthday problem	In probability theory, the birthday paradox states that in a group of 23, or more, randomly chosen people, there is more than 50% probability that some pair of them will have the same birthday. For 57 or more people, the probability is more than 99%, although it cannot be exactly 100% unless there are at least 366 people. This is not a paradox in the sense of leading to a logical contradiction, but is called a paradox because mathematical truth contradicts naive intuition: most people estimate that the chance is much lower than 50%. Calculating the probabilities above is the birthday problem. The mathematics behind it has been used to devise a well-known cryptographic attack named the birthday attack.
Complementary	A pair of angles are complementary if the sum of their angles is 90°.
Odds	In probability theory and statistics the odds in favour of an event or a proposition are the quantity p / 1 − p , where p is the probability of the event or proposition. In other words, an event with m to n odds would have probability m/ m + n.
Mean	The mean, the average in everyday English, which is also called the arithmetic mean (and is distinguished from the geometric mean or harmonic mean). The average is also called the sample mean. The expected value of a random variable, which is also called the population mean.
Check	A check is a negotiable instrument instructing a financial institution to pay a specific amount of a specific currency from a specific demand account held in the maker/depositor face=symbol>¢s name with that institution. Both the maker and payee may be natural persons or legal entities.

Go to **Cram101.com** for the Practice Tests for this Chapter.

Axes	An axes is when two lines intersect somewhere on a plane creating a right angle at intersection
Expression	An expression is a combination of numbers, operators, grouping symbols and/or free variables and bound variables arranged in a meaningful way which can be evaluated..
Circle	In Euclidean geometry, a circle is the set of all points in a plane at a fixed distance, called the radius, from a given point, the center.
Symbols	Symbols are objects, characters, or other concrete representations of ideas, concepts, or other abstractions.
Calculation	A calculation is a deliberate process for transforming one or more inputs into one or more results.
Of the world	The population of the world is the total number of human beings alive on the planet Earth at a given time.
Degree	In mathematics, there are several meanings of degree depending on the subject.
Period	In business, particularly accounting, a period is the time intervals that the accounts, statement, payments, or other calculations cover.
Multiplication	In mathematics, multiplication is an elementary arithmetic operation. When one of the numbers is a whole number, multiplication is the repeated sum of the other number.
Sequence	In mathematics, a sequence is an ordered list of objects. Like a set, it contains members, also called elements or terms, and the number of terms is called the length of the sequence. Unlike a set, order matters, and the exact same elements can appear multiple times at different positions in the sequence.
Segment	In geometry, a line segment is a part of a line that is bounded by two end points, and contains every point on the line between its end points.
Line segment	A line segment is a part of a line that is bounded by two end points, and contains every point on the line between its end points.
Force	In physics, force is an influence that may cause an object to accelerate. It may be experienced as a lift, a push, or a pull. The actual acceleration of the body is determined by the vector sum of all forces acting on it, known as net force or resultant force.

Statistics	Statistics is a mathematical science pertaining to the collection, analysis, interpretation or explanation, and presentation of data. It is applicable to a wide variety of academic disciplines, from the physical and social sciences to the humanities.
Data	Data is a synonym for information.
Average	In mathematics, an average, mean, or central tendency of a data set refers to a measure of the "middle" or "expected" value of the data set.
Interval	In elementary algebra, an interval is a set that contains every real number between two indicated numbers and may contain the two numbers themselves.
Distribution	In mathematical analysis, distribution are objects which generalize functions and probability distributions.
Histogram	In statistics, a histogram is a graphical display of tabulated frequencies.
Bar	The bar (symbol bar) and the millibar (symbol mbar, also mb) are units of pressure.
Frequency	In statistics the frequency of an event i is the number n_i of times the event occurred in the experiment or the study. These frequencies are often graphically represented in histograms.
Degree	In mathematics, there are several meanings of degree depending on the subject.
Conclusion	In a mathematical proof or a syllogism, a conclusion is a statement that is the logical consequence of preceding statements.
Series	A series is the sum of the elements of a sequence.
Limiting	limiting Any process by which a specified characteristic usually amplitude of the output of a device is prevented from exceeding a predetermined value.
Graphs	Graphs are the basic objects of study in graph theory. Informally speaking, a graph is a set of objects called points, nodes, or vertices connected by links called lines or edges.
Of the world	The population of the world is the total number of human beings alive on the planet Earth at a given time.
Meter	The metre (or meter, see spelling differences) is a measure of length. It is the basic unit of length in the metric system and in the International System of Units (SI), used around the world for general and scientific purposes.
Star	In star algebra, a *-ring is an associative ring with an antilinear, antiautomorphism * : A ¨ A which is an involution.
Population	In sociology and biology a population is the collection of people or organisms of a particular species living in a given geographic area or space, usually measured by a census.
Reasoning	Deductive reasoning is the kind of reasoning in which the conclusion is necessitated by, or reached from, previously known facts (the premises).
Code	In mathematical logic, a Gödel numbering (or Gödel code) is a function that assigns to each symbol and well-formed formula of some formal language a unique natural number called its Gödel number.
Communications	Communications are procedures that allow people to exchange information by one of several methods.
Mean	The mean, the average in everyday English, which is also called the arithmetic mean (and is distinguished from the geometric mean or harmonic mean). The average is also called the sample mean. The expected value of a random variable, which is also called the population mean.

Algebra	Algebra is a branch of mathematics concerning the study of structure, relation and quantity.
Sample	sample is a subset of a population.
Column	In mathematics, a matrix can be thought of as each row or column being a vector. Hence, a space formed by row vectors or column vectors are said to be a row space or a column space.
Minor	In linear algebra, a minor of a matrix A is the determinant of some smaller square matrix, cut down from A.
Implication	In logic and mathematics, logical implication is a logical relation that holds between a set T of formulas and a formula B when every model (or interpretation or valuation) of T is also a model of B.
Ring	In mathematics, a ring is an algebraic structure in which addition and multiplication are defined and have properties listed below.
Central	Central is an adjective usually refering to being in the centre.
Central tendency	In mathematics, an average, mean, or central tendency of a data set refers to a measure of the "middle" or "expected" value of the data set.
Gross pay	Gross pay is a form of periodic payment from an employer to an employee, which is specified in an employment contract.
Salary	A salary is a form of periodic payment from an employer to an employee, which is specified in an employment contract.
Median	In probability theory and statistics, a median is a number dividing the higher half of a sample, a population, or a probability distribution from the lower half.
Mode	In statistics, mode means the most frequent value assumed by a random variable, or occurring in a sampling of a random variable.
Measure	A measure is a function that assigns a number to subsets of a given set.
Volume	The volume of a solid object is the three-dimensional concept of how much space it occupies, often quantified numerically.
Rate	A rate is a special kind of ratio, indicating a relationship between two measurements with different units, such as miles to gallons or cents to pounds.
Colorado	The State of Colorado is a state located in the Rocky Mountain region of the United States of America.
Period	In business, particularly accounting, a period is the time intervals that the accounts, statement, payments, or other calculations cover.
Element	An element or member of a set is an object that when collected together make up the set.
Measurement	Measurement is the estimation of a physical quantity such as distance, energy, temperature, or time.
Axes	An axes is when two lines intersect somewhere on a plane creating a right angle at intersection
Classes	In set theory and its applications throughout mathematics, classes are a collection of sets (or sometimes other mathematical objects) that can be unambiguously defined by a property that all its members share.
Pairs	In mathematics, the conjugate pairs or adjoint matrix of an m-by-n matrix A with complex entries is the n-by-m matrix A* obtained from A by taking the transpose and then taking the complex conjugate of each entry.

Go to **Cram101.com** for the Practice Tests for this Chapter.

Scale	In Euclidean geometry, a uniform scale is a linear transformation that enlargers or diminishes objects, and whose scale factor is the same in all directions. This is also called homothethy.
Amount	amount is a kind of property which exists as magnitude or multitude. It is among the basic classes of things along with quality, substance, change, and relation.
Martin Gardner	Martin Gardner (b. October 21, 1914, Tulsa, Oklahoma) is a popular American mathematics and science writer specializing in recreational mathematics, but with interests encompassing magic (conjuring), pseudoscience, literature (especially Lewis Carroll), philosophy, and religion.
Range	In mathematics, the range of a function is the set of all "output" values produced by that function. Given a function f :A $\rightarrow$ B, the range of class="unicode">f, is defined to be the set {x class="unicode"> B:x= class="unicode">f(a) for some a class="unicode"> A}.
Standard deviation	standard deviation of a probability distribution, random variable, or population or multiset of values is a measure of the spread of its values.
Deviation	Deviation is a measure of difference for interval and ratio variables between the observed value and the mean.
Square	In plane geometry, a square is a polygon with four equal sides, four right angles, and parallel opposite sides. In algebra, the square of a number is that number multiplied by itself.
Square root	In mathematics, a square root of a number x is a number r such that r^2 = x, or in words, a number r whose square (the result of multiplying the number by itself) is x.
Root	In mathematics, a root of a complex-valued function f is a member x of the domain of f such that f(x) vanishes at x, that is, x : f (x) = 0.
Curve	In mathematics, the concept of a curve tries to capture the intuitive idea of a geometrical one-dimensional and continuous object. A simple example is the circle.
Midpoint	midpoint is the middle point of a line segment.
Axis	An axis is a straight line around which a geometric figure can be rotated.
Horizontal	In astronomy, geography, geometry and related sciences and contexts, a plane is said to be horizontal at a given point if it is locally perpendicular to the gradient of the gravity field, i.e., with the direction of the gravitational force at that point.
Sum	A sum is the result of the addition of a set of numbers. The numbers may be natural numbers, complex numbers, matrices, or still more complicated objects. An infinite sum is a subtle procedure known as a series.
Abraham De Moivre	Abraham De Moivre was a French mathematician famous for de Moivre's formula, which links complex numbers and trigonometry, and for his work on the normal distribution and probability theory.
Probability	Probability is the chance that something is likely to happen or be the case.
Binomial	In elementary algebra, a binomial is a polynomial with two terms: the sum of two monomials. It is the simplest kind of polynomial except for a monomial.
Binomial	Binomial probability typically deals with the probability of several successive decisions,

Go to **Cram101.com** for the Practice Tests for this Chapter.

probability	each of which has two possible outcomes.
Test	Acid test ratio measures the ability of a company to use its near cash or quick assets to immediately extinguish its current liabilities.
Mile	A mile is a unit of length, usually used to measure distance, in a number of different systems, including Imperial units, United States customary units and Norwegian/Swedish mil. Its size can vary from system to system, but in each is between 1 and 10 kilometers. In contemporary English contexts mile refers to either:
Curves	In mathematics, curves are the intuitive idea of a geometrical one-dimensional and continuous object.
Units	The units of measurement are a globally standardized and modernized form of the metric system.
Temperature	Temperature is a physical property of a system that underlies the common notions of hot and cold; something that is hotter has the greater temperature.
Insurance	Insurance, in law and economics, is a form of risk management primarily used to hedge against the risk of a contingent loss.
Whole number	In mathematics, a whole number can mean either an element of the set {1, 2, 3, ...} (i.e the positive integers) or an element of the set {0, 1, 2, 3, ...} (i.e. the non-negative integers).
Rounding	Rounding is the process of reducing the number of significant digits in a number.
Circle	In Euclidean geometry, a circle is the set of all points in a plane at a fixed distance, called the radius, from a given point, the center.
Network	In Graph theory, a network is a digraph with weighted edges.
Pyramid	An n-sided pyramid is a polyhedron formed by connecting an n-sided polygonal base and a point, called the apex, by n triangular faces. In other words, it is a conic solid with polygonal base.
Consecutive	Consecutive means in succession or back-to-back
Experiment	In the scientific method, an experiment (Latin: ex-+-periri, "of (or from) trying"), is a set of actions and observations, performed in the context of solving a particular problem or question, in order to support or falsify a hypothesis or research concerning phenomena.
Drawings	Drawings (i.e. Plans) are a set of two-dimensional diagrams or drawings used to describe a place or object, or to communicate building or fabrication instructions.
Light	Light is electromagnetic radiation with a wavelength that is visible to the eye (visible light) or, in a technical or scientific context, electromagnetic radiation of any wavelength.
Proper	A proper fraction is a fraction in which the absolute value of the numerator is less than the denominator--hence, the absolute value of the fraction is less than 1.
Universe	The Universe is defined as the summation of all particles and energy that exist and the space-time which all events occur.
Determining	Determining the expected value of a random variable displays the average or central value of the variable.It is a summary value of the distribution of the variable.
Sampling	Sampling is the part of statistical practice concerned with the selection of individual observations intended to yield some knowledge about a population of concern, especially for the purposes of statistical inference.
Music	Multiple Signal Classification, also known as MUSIC, is an algorithm used for frequency

Go to Cram101.com for the Practice Tests for this Chapter.

estimation and emitter location.

Epidemic	In epidemiology, an epidemic is a disease that appears as new cases in a given human population, during a given period, at a rate that substantially exceeds with is "expected," based on recent experience.
Empty	In mathematics and more specifically set theory, the empty set is the unique set which contains no elements.
Grouping	In abstract algebra, grouping consists of sets with binary operations that satisfy certain axioms.
Health	Health is the level of functional and/or metabolic efficiency of an organism at both the micro level.
Product	In mathematics, a product is the result of multiplying, or an expression that identifies factors to be multiplied.
Force	In physics, force is an influence that may cause an object to accelerate. It may be experienced as a lift, a push, or a pull. The actual acceleration of the body is determined by the vector sum of all forces acting on it, known as net force or resultant force.
Valid	In statistics, a valid measure is one which is measuring what is supposed to measure.
Check	A check is a negotiable instrument instructing a financial institution to pay a specific amount of a specific currency from a specific demand account held in the maker/depositor face=symbol>¢s name with that institution. Both the maker and payee may be natural persons or legal entities.
Minutes	Minutes are a measure of time.
Percent	percent is a way of expressing a number as a fraction of 100 per cent meaning "per hundred".
Discount	In finance and economics, discount is the process of finding the present value of an amount of cash at some future date, and along with compounding cash forms the basis of time value of money calculations.
Bar graph	A bar chart, also known as a bar graph, is a chart with rectangular bars of lengths usually proportional to the magnitudes or frequencies of what they represent.

Leaves	Horizontal axis of display containing the trailing digits is called leaves.
Mean	The most important measure of central tendency, and one of the basic building blocks of all statistical analysis, is the arithmetic mean. It is simply the sum of all the set of values divided by the number of values involved. As a measure of central tendency, it is affected by extreme scores, and it assumes a ratio scale of measurement.
Power	The probability of correctly rejecting a false Ho is referred to as power.
Probability	A probability provides a quantitative description of the likely occurrence of a particular event. Probability is conventionally expressed on a scale from 0 to 1; a rare event has a probability close to 0, a very common event has a probability close to 1. Probability is calculated as the ratio of the number of favorable events to the total number of possible events.
Relationships	One major objective of statistical analysis is the identification of associations or relationships that exist between and among sets of observations. In other words, does knowledge about about one set of data allow us to infer or predict characteristics about another set or sets of data.
Experiment	An experiment is any process or study, which results in the collection of data, the outcome of which is unknown. In statistics, the term is usually restricted to situations in which the researcher has control over some of the conditions under which the experiment takes place.
Objects	Objects refer to any data source, whether individuals, physical or biological things, geographic locations, time periods, or events; that is, anything upon which observations can be made.
Scale	A scale is a scheme for the numerical representation of the values of a variable. The interpretation we place upon the numbers of the scale, rather than the numbers themselves, makes the scale useful. The most common scales are nominal, ordinal, interval
Factor	Factor is used synonymously for variable.

CPSIA information can be obtained at www.ICGtesting.com
Printed in the USA
LVOW091547040912

297321LV00001B/90/A